INNOVATION
MAGIC

Innovation Magic

The science and art of Innovation Management

Reena Dayal

PARTRIDGE
A Penguin Random House Company

Print information available on the last page.

To order additional copies of this book, contact
Partridge India
000 800 10062 62
orders.india@partridgepublishing.com

www.partridgepublishing.com/india

Contents

INTRODUCTION

The holy grail of the Innovation Function in an Organization is to keep the spirit of Intrapreneurship alive within the Organization, even when the Organization grows in size, expanding and becoming more and more unwieldy (if not bureaucratic). This of course raises the following questions:

1. How does one identify the true Innovators in a large Organization and then harness them for the cause of Innovation?
2. How should the Organizational Innovation function be structured to make all of this happen?
3. How does one create a Culture for Innovation so that Innovation and it's enabling processes begin to work on their own?

This book attempts to answer these three questions and while there is an attempt to answer these in order, you will often see that the answers overlap and more than one question gets discussed /addressed at the same time. There is also an exploration of the role that artists may have to play in Business and Technology innovations. The role of the Specialist Generalist has been used to understand important ingredients for collaborative Innovation in today's business environment. Read the book as an Introduction to these subjects. It is intended to be a reference for Innovation Management Evangelists in Organizations and for every person in the Organization who believes "Innovation is Everybody's Responsibility" not just that of a specific function in the Organization. This is not a reference book for acquiring deep technical knowledge, but something you can breeze through and let the learnings seep through your thoughts, and emerge as common sense in the way that you deal with Innovation. So happy reading......

Creativity And Innovation

Some gifted adventurer is always sailing round
the world of art and science, to bring home
costly merchandise from every port.
[— Robert Aris Willmott

Identifying and Harnessing the Explorers

INNOVATION, INTUITION, EXPLORERS AND ARTISTS

"These are the voyages of the starship *Enterprise*. Its five-year mission: to explore strange new worlds, to seek out new life and new civilizations, to boldly go where no man has gone before." These legendary words (Captain's Oath) from the Star Trek are a favorite amongst the true explorers in this world. When we examine the characteristics of innovators, they are like explorers seeking out new meaning, new solutions and learning from new experiences. They even learn new things from old experiences, boldly trying what has not been tried before. They think out of the box and create and invent solutions, thereby harness the human potential. Through the explorers in this world, we are exposed to "the power of the human mind".

Organizations need strong explorers, but they also need these explorers to work together in a manner, that their collectiveness is a more powerful problem solving and creativity machine than the sum of their individual capability. This Collective Intelligence is the key to Collaborative Innovation and for multitude of ideas/solutions to emerge. Every Innovation practitioner * and by that I mean somebody who holds direct responsibility for

Innovation in an Organization, is on a constant lookout for people who are the true explorers.

Explorers are people who can sense the landscape of the market and identify opportunities that make the biggest impact for the Organization. These explorers seem to have the unique trait of identifying very different insights than most others, when exposed to the same set of information. It is therefore not a co-incidence that many people similar to me, try to think of ways and means of identifying and nurturing the existing explorers. We also attempt to groom potential explorers. This is a challenging task and requires a deeper dive into how the mind of an explorer works and hence all this fascination with the working of the human mind.

The most remarkable trait of outstanding new ideas/ associated innovations is that they emerge as correlations or combinations of existing stuff and in many cases the idea actually seems extremely intuitive to the person who puts forward the idea. Steve Jobs had once said "I found that there were these incredibly great people at work doing certain things, and that you couldn't replace one of these people with fifty average people. They could just do things that no number of average people could do" I couldn't agree more with that statement based on my own observations within the Organizational context.

When you ask Innovative people, as to how they reached certain conclusions, or came up with certain ideas, they have a hard time explaining the same. The creativity displayed by Innovative people is clear and visible, however how they are creative and what makes them more creative is sometimes a mystery. Even more mysterious is the method by which they can sometimes jump to conclusions. This jumping to conclusions (often correct conclusions) is akin to being intuitive.

Understanding this phenomenon is the "Holy Grail" of Innovation Nurturing and Management. Hence a tremendous amount of interest in how the human mind works.

Daniel Kahnemann talks about the "Two Systems" working within the Human brain - in his book" Thinking Fast and Slow" My interpretation of Kahnemann's concepts helps me understand the Intuitive Innovator a bit better. System 1 as per Kahnemann is the intuitive Brain and System 2 is the Logical, Rational, Cognitive brain.

While all individuals have both systems functioning within them, both seem to have a mind of their own. However when we examine a specific act or activity by and Individual, it may be dominated by System 1 or System 2.

Now it seems that Intuitive thinking can be enhanced by adding more food for thought to the brain. If there is enough knowledge stored in the brain for a particular subject or associated areas, and these are being recalled on a regular basis (as for a practitioner), then there are several pathways that are pre-established in the brain. Every time the subject is recalled in a specific new context, new pathways are triggered, which may result in new correlations or identification of new patterns related to the subject.

Most of this processing happens automatically and sometimes multiple correlations and patterns are processed by the subconscious internally so that the answer or solution just seems to jump out of the blue. This is a somewhat simplistic explanation from a scientific perspective, however from an organizational perspective gives useful insights. This gives important pointers to identify explorers.

Understanding how intuition works may lead us to understand the essential components for High Value Intuition and also identification of parameters, environmental factors, learning techniques and experiences that fast track such intuitiveness. One key aspect of this intuition is that one should have some depth in Subject Matter Knowledge (practitioner)

The combination of the power of the subconscious mind and the Rational Thinking mind creates Innovative Solutions relevant and practical and observable by the society, industry etc.

There are some generic and common traits across the explorers which are worthy of note.

- They exhibit curiosity
- They challenge assumptions
- Have trained their mind to think beyond the realms of existing assumptions.

Let us examine the Curiosity Trait a little in detail.

Curiosity

Most Explorers have a naturally curious mind. They ask questions to satisfy their curiosity and get answers that may lead to new correlations in their mind. Very often cultural conditioning or lack of confidence on the subject or plain hesitance refrains people from asking questions that could be critical to ensure more innovative Problem Solving.

As human beings we are least conditioned on this aspect when we are kids. When a child is one or two years old, the learning happens at a phenomenal rate and continues that way for a few more years. The rate of learning (on an average) slows down as we grow older. There are several factors associated with this, however one of the factors is definitely the amount of curiosity we exhibit. If you examine the behaviour of a small child, few very salient points emerge

1. No Question is so stupid that it cannot be asked! Children ask questions nonstop
2. When children think, there are no assumptions. So boundaries of thinking are not impacted by pre-set moulds or assumptions
3. For a child –"everything is possible"

These are all good traits to follow for Innovation. An additional point to be kept in mind is that Correlations in the brain happen based on the information that is stored in the brain- so from an Organizational Context, Subject Matter Knowledge is important. The more knowledge on a subject the better the chances of creating more correlation points to derive new inferences and deduce new approaches to Solutions.

How do we train our minds to think out of the box

Each brain comes with its own unique set of environmental influences, exposure, learning and its own unique mechanism of assimilation.

Since every individual has a certain set way of looking at things, we can now begin to examine the ways in which the set way of thinking can be altered. If we can consciously alter the approach to thinking we may be able to come up with new ideas. The stimulus to think differently can be created artificially. To understand this let us consider the following example- In solving simple puzzles like "Where does 4 fit in the following series

"11, 5, 15, 16, 10, 29, 22"? When trying to solve this, most people would look at the kind of number series that is evolving and any associated patterns. The answer really strikes you if you try speaking the numbers aloud. Try- eleven, five, fifteen, sixteen, ten twenty nine and twenty two- When you speak aloud these numbers, it quickly strikes that the series is alphabetical.

It seems that the moment we start thinking from an entirely different perspective, the answer is staring in the face.

In this example the external stimulus for thinking differently came from speaking the words out aloud. This is not very difficult to understand scientifically as well, since the auditory data is interpreted by a very different part of the brain.

A Corollary to this is the following" If we can train our brain to think through multiple departure points in the brain and through different techniques, then our ability to creatively solve problems increases"

We discussed that forcing your brain to think from multiple departure points helps create alternate scenarios to address a particular problem statement. This in turn leads to different correlation patterns in the brain (leverage existing and create new ones).

So the question is, how do we train our brains to think differently? Here are some simple ways used extensively during problem solving. The trick is to try multiple of them when you want alternate solutions or need to think differently.

1. Visualization- Problems that have multiple components to be understood, become simpler to attack if the theory is converted into diagrams or represented pictorially in some form. There is a reason why most technical people rush to use the whiteboard during almost every discussion. This is again linked to providing different stimulus to the brain while trying to solve the same problem

2. Discussion- Speaking the problem aloud and then "Thinking Aloud" the possible solutions and associated pros, cons etc. This was explained in the example of speaking aloud the number series

3. Use of special techniques that allow you to see every point of view associated with the problem. "What

if Analysis "and Six Thinking Hats by Edward De Bono are some good techniques for the same

4. Forcing your brain to correlate. This can be done by picking up a "random word" and systematically correlating it to your problem statement till it starts making sense. Sounds absurd...you have to try this technique out to realize the power and potential of the same

5. Getting a multidisciplinary team working on the same problem. If you are solving a science and Technology Problem, might be useful to involve some right brainers or Artists in the same as well.

Creativity and Innovation–Nugget No1a: Knowledge centric Intuition is important for Business. Use techniques to promote intuitive and "out of the box" thinking

Creativity and Innovation–Nugget No1b: Curiosity is an important trait for creativity

Multidisciplinary learning and the role of Artists

We tend to think of Science and Technology being subjects close to each other and Art as a distinct subject belonging to the "Right Brainers" of the world. Yet most people who are engaged in creative problem solving in science and technology need as much of the right brains creative and imaginative thinking as any artist.

The design of technology today is no longer bound to the realms of bits, bytes and mechanical or process design concepts. This is the age of the artists. In some senses the technologists are artists too. Take the example of Steve Jobs, he was an artist in the sense that he challenged traditional conventional thinking about user interfaces and introduced revolutionary new designs to the world.

Hyundai came out with an ad which said "Artnnovation" (Art + Innovation) for their i10 campaign in India. The ad claimed that the Car had been developed jointly by artists and technologists.

The Nano "Art in Motion" campaign leverages artists to paint their fantasies on the Innovative nano. Another example of Art and Innovation for Technology.

The automotive examples are somewhat intuitive, since design and aesthetics is one of the key elements of the appeal of the automobile to the masses, of course coupled with the actual engine quality and performance. At the same time, there are non-intuitive examples as well. A company called Littlebits sells lego like electronic components for building larger electronic solutions. The driving factor for the concept it seems came as much from the Art and Design background of the founder as it did from the engineering and technology mindset.

This topic has moved from the realms of experiments to serious application There are Organizations today that promote education and networking across Science, Technology and Art such as Leonardo Publications.

The following is a list of some interesting art and technology mixed solutions

- Location aware music, which may hold the key to solving cognitive disorders http://www.ted.com/talks/ryan_holladay_to_hear_this_music_you_have_to_be_there_literally

   The concept is based on tagging contextual music composed for the landscape with the location itself. This was done by creating a location aware album for Central Park in New York. You use an app and as you move around Park, you keep hearing the music associated with the various segments of the park that you traverse. In case you re-traverse the park through a different path, you hear a different sequence of the music. The app creates a completely different way for people to interact with the landscape and the music.

- Cymatics creates beautiful patterns from sound http://www.dvice.com/2013-6-10/video-day-sound-waves-create-mesmerizing-patterns-sand

   When a tone generator is connected to a metal plate and sand is placed on the plate, interesting things happen. The sand creates frequency specific geometric designs and vibrations tone undergoes a change.

- Artists are helping identify patterns in big data by applying non conventional methods and helping reach meaningful insightful conclusions with the data as was the case of the EnglaID project.

The entire mixing process more or less started with Artistic representation of complex scientific scenarios to generate interest in the common man, but the real potential lies in Artists and Scientists working together to create more discoveries inventions for humankind.'

Art as a representation of the research in science

An exhibition that aims to blur the boundaries between art and science was on display at the Imperial College, London. The exhibition was showcasing work produced through the collaboration of staff and students from the Imperial College, The Royal College of Art, Central St Martin's and the Courtauld Institute of Art. The exhibition included pieces exploring a wide range of scientific interests, from Heisenberg's uncertainty principle through group theory to fungal infections in plants

The Leonardo International Society for the Arts, Science and Technology (ISAST) is trying to provide a context for the discussion of the contemporary practices, ideas and frameworks in the arena where art and science connect.

"Information Arts- Intersection of Art, Science and Technology" by Stephen Wilson and promoted by the Leonardo society explores science and technology as Cultural contexts for the current world and the role that artists can play in creating and envisioning future possibilities. This can only happen when they interface with the current research and understand it at the level that an artist needs to understand.

University of Texas at Dallas has a unique Arts and Technology Program This program merges the Innovation Process of Artists, Scientists and Engineers, exploring experimental models through new technologies. It augments the study of the arts and humanities by engagement with the research tools, measures and practices of science and technology. They also have a program which focuses on the uses and impact of technology for communication, culture and commerce.

In the next few pages I have included a few anecdotal learnings around interactions with artists and how their way of thinking can impact an engineering /technical thinking environment

Creativity and Innovation—Nugget No 2: The boundaries of science and art and those between subjects are blurring. Recognize this and introduce counterintuitive subject matter expertise into the solutioning discussion to get remarkable results

Some anecdotal learnings

Blurring of Boundaries

During a leadership course in Innovation at Oxford we had a lecture by Miranda Creswell on "Cezanne, peripheral vision and traversing scale" an eye opening session into interpretation of art. This was followed by a tour of the Cezanne exhibition at the Ashmolean museum...seeing for reality the theory taught in the lecture. The discussion shifted to "blurring of boundaries" since this is the technique that Cezanne applied in his art and created remarkable three dimensional depth in his paintings. The topic struck a chord, since I have written in the past on the Blurring of Boundaries in business - http://sites.tcs.com/innovation-forum/reminiscences-from-the-forum-the-flight-of-the-butterfly.

My takeaway- A reaffirmation of my beliefs that analogies in art apply to science and technology. What an artist gets intuitively, science explains through theory and technologists find ways to replicate!

Interestingly Miranda is working on a project which is using big data to interpret the Landscapes of England, a project called EnglaID. A wonderful case of art and science working together with technology. Apparently one of the advantages of having artists involved in the project is that they make pattern recognition within landscape changes easier and then the same can be corroborated with actual data.

Art is subject to multiple interpretations and hence makes allowances for differences in thinking styles, opinions and interpretations. Art is also concerned with patterns, patterns that represent the style of an artist, patterns that are associated with and used to interpret an object or a landscape. Look closely at these qualities and it becomes evident that when we blur the boundaries between subjects, we create opportunities for analogous rapid learning and creating new solutions.

The educational basis of learning any subject is extremely similar around the world- truer for science and technology than in the arts, where local (country/regional) influences can sometimes dictate /promote a different path of learning. Due to the kind of interconnectivity that exists today, the observations by scientific /research communities are shared at a phenomenal rate. Therefore two very different groups working on the same technology have a very high likelihood of coming up with the same possible next steps. When we mix Art with Science and Technology, we are dealing with unknown/less known patterns and hence the level of creativity in deriving solutions, and the newness of the solutions that may emerge may be extraordinarily high.

An artist can intuitively imagine scenarios/patterns which can then be matched to science and technology scenarios and create possibilities and solutions that were not thought of before

In that sense, when we blur the boundary lines of traditional subject types and use that approach in problem solving we may get some remarkable results.

In some senses when Steve Jobs created the iPhone he was thinking more like an artist, it was only later that the tech solutionist in him took over. So an Engineer/Technologist has much to learn from and apply as far as art is concerned.

The Many Possibilities

Another examples of what engineers can learn from other disciplines came through during an archaeological visit to Avebury- a historical site from the new stone age period. Avebury is around 25 miles from Stonehenge. Stonehenge is a more popularly known pre-historic site. I had lots of questions around the site and being an Engineer by education was quickly amazed at the fact that Archaeologists can be happy with "Many possible explanations" associated with the site artifacts and how they happened to get there. The fact that over time more information may get uncovered and the interpretations may change, get added to, was also apparently fine. I obviously had a lot of questions, but finally got the answer when we were taking a break and having coffee at a local café. There were fourteen of us – Twelve Indians and two professors from Oxford. One of the Professors said "Reena, we may be able to address your concern around lack of finality - finally. Think of this way... all of us sitting around these two tables in this café and a volcano erupts nearby and we are all immediately trapped in the lava and hence preserved with our surroundings. Assuming that several tens of thousands of year later, and assuming that no written records are discovered alongside, people would find these fourteen individuals seemingly having some drinks together. A further analysis would reveal that twelve seems to be foreign to the location while two are aboriginals. What was this, they may wonder? A social get together, a ritual exercise, random people sitting in a café? Archaeologists will spend a lot of time thinking of these options, yet what are the chances that they would jump to the conclusion that this was a group of twelve Indians for a site visit and two Professors from Oxford. Without written records supporting this situation, there is no way for anyone to find out what really happened."

Engineers tend to be problem solvers. Problem? no problem, let's work on the solution...and that's how inventions have happened and science has progressed and we live the life that we do today. However we all know that Innovativeness is not merely about problem solving. Humans are hard wired intrinsically to seek beyond the obvious and to look for opportunities where there are none. Possibly the most important breakthroughs have come from "Not thinking like an Engineer", but by considering the abstract to seek out alternate scenarios and to look for explanations which may challenge all that may have been proven till now. This is what scientists in the realm of theoretical physics are trying to do. This is also how possibly the first critical inventions of the world "the wheel" and "the discovery of fire" came into being.

In business, when we look at the long term evolution of market and the nature in which business boundaries are likely to blur across industries over a period of time, it is a little like considering many possibilities and then placing a bet on one of them while taking decisions for the business you are responsible for. If you are doing this, chances are each step of your life is like an archaeologist, working with limited information and trying to reach conclusions while drawing learning's from the past and then use this information to foresee the future.

In this era of Big Data, you may turn around and disagree. I would then request you to consider this "Solving a Big Data Problem today is like solving an Archaeology problem. A lot depends on how much data you have collected about the past, how much of that can be trusted and whether you have got the relationship between multiple data elements, sources correctly established."

Yet big data as a technology is extremely exciting in the possibilities that it offers. I think the real merit of big data will be evident in the days to come. Today with the revolution happening in the Internet of Things, more and more data will be collected at the source of the data generation, by machines. The authenticity of this data will be higher and as we move forward, this data will yield useful analytics from the past, which can be used reliably to predict the future. Patient health data captured minute by minute (if the disease so requires) in the convenience of wherever the patient is, will yield analytics which will enable preventive intervention. Preventive maintenance of Infrastructure, preventive maintenance in factories, all will yield huge benefits not just from a cost perspective but in saving lives as well.

While big data coupled with Analytics and enabled by Internet of Things (IOT) will yield wonderful solutions, there will still be many areas where there will never be enough information to be 100% sure of any decision making. Human beings will end up being provided by lots of data and analysis and faced with the challenge of more and more complex decision making. So each Leader has and will continue to wear two hats - that of an engineer (who keeps things on course) and that of the visionary who foresees and enables the future!

<u>Creativity and Innovation—Nugget No 3: Innovators in Technology can learn from Art and Archaeology. Learning from other subjects can be applied to problem solving in a different subject</u>

Challenging Presumptions

One day, a group of people at Oxford had punts reserved from the College Boathouse. A punt is a small flat boat that is manoeuvred on slightly shallow waters with the help of a pole. The pole is usually fourteen feet long and quite heavy. As it turned out everybody was in a hurry in the group to try out punting and around six people went onto the first boat. When it came to the second round three of us were left, all of us Engineers by education. The moment we took off, our wonderful friends on the shore (Architect, Artists, Fund Manager, Consultants) could be seen smiling and shaking their heads "All engineers aboard, you will spend half the time theorizing and designing the most optimum way to make the boat move!!" To our chagrin, we did start going round in circles, and yes, at least one of us was very keen to get the theory right! Oops and now we were being watched!

By the end of the one and half hour session though we were enjoying a near perfect punting experience amidst the beautiful natural greenery in Oxford. So what happened? - We actually discovered wonderful leadership reminders during that day.

1. Initially when we were going round in circles and there seemed to be some pressure to get it right, One of my colleagues asked the question "Hey come on- Are we having fun? and just as he said this, a portion of the boat went under some overgrowth along the banks of the river and we made complete spectacles of ourselves half embedded in shrubs, (the only more funny thing that happens is when somebody

just topples off the boat or is left hanging to the pole while the boat moves on). At that point we just doubled up laughing at ourselves. Somehow that changed our approach to the process completely.... and by focussing on enjoying the learning of "how to steer and manage the boat" we removed the pressure of presumptions from our minds

2. One thing that we discovered pretty quickly was that I could not manage the Pole for thrust for long durations, since I would tire quickly handling that heavy pole. My male colleagues on the boat were better at that. We also discovered that I was the best though at steering the boat through tricky corners and when we had vegetation looming over parts of the river. We just took turns accordingly...(we exhibited good teamwork)

3. We did end up having a great time that day! Life, Work and learning are truly intermingled. Analogies from work apply to life and everyday situations in life are opportunities to innovate, to learn to draw from learning from anywhere...there are no boundaries to learning. Presumptions and stereotypes are the biggest roadblocks to being innovative, for finding new and different solutions. Similarly lessons from everyday life are big lessons to be applied at work.

Creativity and Innovation—Nugget No 4: Get rid of presumptions, expand your thinking, leverage team work and also look for learning from all around.

Fast tracking Learning from Analogy

Learning from Analogy is an important aspect of fast tracking learning. We need more Specialist Generalists today (or Thought Integrators as I call them). From a multiple subject perspective or a generalist perspective they need to be able to understand multiple perspectives and pick up new subjects very quickly so that they can correlate to the subject and actually use this knowledge to envisage new solutions. In a conversation with a colleague we discussed how some people may remember some incidents from their early childhood in great details, but may not be able to recall clearly something that happened a few years ago. It seems that the quality of experience and the importance that we associate with the experience defines how we store the memory associated with the experience/event. This surely has a role to play in learning as well. When unconventional correlation is setup for thinking around a subject, learning it becomes simpler. Half of the Tech world today seeks inspiration for new ideas from popular science fiction literature and movies around the world. Pranav Mistry- the famous inventor of the Sixth sense solutions has been inspired by Mythology he says. Lot of products today have actual artists working on designs that are more user friendly. Humans have understood that the efficiency of the design of biological systems is so advanced from any systems invented by man, that today there is a tremendous amount of research that is happening to understand how different biological systems work and bio mimicry is a science by itself. This is especially true in the areas of cognitive systems and artificial intelligence. But the applications of biomimicry and learning from nature are varied and impacting areas as diverse and vast as Agriculture, Architecture, Climate Change, Energy, Industrial Design, Medicine, Pollution handling, Transportation and Robotics.

In Praise of Air

In Praise of Air' is a poem which is displayed on the Alfred Denny Building at the University of Sheffield, UK until May 2015. The poem was the idea of Tony Ryan, Professor of Physical Chemistry and the Pro-Vice Chancellor of the Faculty of Science at the University of Sheffield. They created the material of the banner on which the poem is printed. This material, it is claimed can remove the nitrogen oxide pollution created by 20 cars every day. The material is based on revolutionary nano technology.

This concept of materials that can interact with the environment to create positive results, has given rise to several new projects One is around Catalytic Clothing http://www.catalytic-clothing.org, which aims to develop clothes and textiles that can act as a catalytic surface to purify air. This is a perfect example of using an existing technology in a remarkably new way. While lot of this is in the experimental stage and early piloting, I am confident that this technology has the capacity to bring about a revolution of sorts. Catalytic Clothing is a partnership between The University of Sheffield, University of the Arts London and London College of Fashion

Examples from Nature

Another example from nature is the Lotus plant which keeps it's leaves clean despite growing in muddy environments. The ridges and the tiny bumps on the leaves keep water droplets from spreading across the surface. As a result, the water beads and slides away, carrying particles of dirt with it. Developers have applied this lotus effect to paint. When the paint dries, tiny bumps remain on the surface that help water droplets remove dirt.

One of the most well known and most popular and simple example of bio mimicry is the Velcro, which was inspired by the clinging capacity of the burdock burrs.

An Engineering example from bio mimicry is the design of the high speed trains in Japan where the engineers succeeded in reducing the noise levels by adapting to the design of the pantographs (Current collector) to the shape of the serrations on an owls wing. The same trains adopted one more insight for noise reduction from the kingfisher. Entry and Exit of these high speed trains into tunnels would be accompanied by an explosive noise. The engineers observed he kingfisher and it's zero noise, zero ripple entry into the water for catching fish. It seems the design of the kingfisher's beak specially enables this to happen. They derived the design of the front of the train on the same model and achieved remarkable results.

The concept of zero waste architectures and ecosystems today is based on biomimicry of not just one organism but entire natural ecosystems. The Sahara Forest Project is a good example of such a scenario. The project combines saltwater cooled greenhouses with Solar power technologies, either directly using Photovoltaic or indirectly using Concentrated Solar Power and technologies for desert re vegetation. The attempt is to create a sustainable and profitable source of energy, food, vegetation and water. Currently some pilot projects are happening in Jordon and Qatar with very encouraging results.

The red sea weed inspired approach to controlling bacteria might help provide effective solutions for stopping bacteria from being harmful, while preventing new strains of antibiotic resistant bacteria from forming. The Red seaweed (Delisea pulchra), is surprisingly free of biofilms as opposed to several other plants which grow in the water. It does so by secreting chemicals which are very similar to the signalling molecules that the bacteria use. These serve to disrupt the communication mechanism amongst the bacteria and prevents the bacteria from forming colonies. So the bacteria themselves are not killed, but they do not form biofilms which may cause them to become virulent.

And back to the Artists, anecdotal learning through Analogy

In a 3 hour drive from Oxford to Cambridge, I had a reasonably long conversation with an Artist about "Blurring of Boundaries" It was an interesting conversation, talking about the concept within the framework of Art and Archaeology and I talking in the context of business and both of us also talking about this subject in the philosophical

/metaphysical context. It was one of the most amazing discussions that I have had.

The most amazing aspect of the discussion was that we talked about "Blurring of Boundaries" in many possible contexts. This was a conversation between an artist and an Electronics Engineer by Education and an IT professional. Our conversation was beautifully derived from one analogy to another. Today in the digital age, the boundaries are blurring between businesses massively …competition can come from any market segment. What would you call Apple – A devices Company? What about Google? When Netflix started operations, who would have thought that Blockbuster would go bust, but it did. Similarly Apple took away the complete market share from the leader Blackberry in a a mere 1.5 years and now the iPhone6 is a health monitoring device as well. Cable companies are providing internet today and Media Content Providers are trying to become the channel as well, eliminating the intermediaries.

The discussion quickly shifted to How Cezanne used the technique of blurred boundaries to give 3 dimensional depth to objects. The topic shifted to landscapes and how boundaries in landscapes blur with time and merge and reform. So in a sense if one creates a view of the landscape changes over a time cycle, very interesting historical facts may get revealed.

Then the topic shifted to how boundaries define societies and lives, boundaries of states, boundaries of religions and boundaries of beliefs. Collaboration and openness requires a little bit of blurring of these boundaries…and I could not but help correlate this with how Companies work together to create Industry Best Practices through Industry Forums and Standard Bodies..When a group of companies work together on a Standard, the individual boundaries of these organizational existence are a little blurred within the context of the Industry Forum participation on Standard creation. These Forums do play and important part in the context of the Innovation Ecosystem of an Organization and hence the example seems relevant to include here.

We also talked about the ultimate boundary that exists, that between life and death, but that part of the conversation is probably more relevant for a different type of book.

Creativity and Innovation–Nugget No 5: Multidisciplinary knowledge requires some knowledge across multiple subjects. Learning through analogy can help fast track learning in new subjects and analogy derived solutions can be extremely unique and innovative

Innovation Management

[The building blocks add one by one
To create the total, the total sum
Yet as you take a block away
The frame should at the most sway
[Reena Dayal]

Building the Innovative Organization

Organizational Building Blocks for Innovation

Steve Jobs once said "So when a good idea comes, you know, part of my job is to move it around, just see what different people think, get people talking about it, argue with people about it, get ideas moving among that group of 100 people, get different people together to explore different aspects of it quietly, and, you know – just explore things."

While this statement talks about the role of a good innovative idea, it also highlights the importance of the fact that there may be multiple smaller ideas hidden within the grand implementation plan of the master idea, and there is an equal need to discover these smaller ideas as one moves forward. This is the reason why Innovation within an Organization needs a special environment for new ideas to be implemented.

There is a tremendous amount of conversation in the corporate world today about Intrapreneurship and of course one may argue that Innovation is an overused word, yet there has been very little talk around the mechanisms that could enable such Intrapreneurship and Innovation within a large Corporate Environment.

Processes are good. I come from a process and a technology background and early on in my career I realized that Organizational efficiency is dependent on well-honed processes. The innovation side of me though does realize that agility is much more important in an Entrepreneurial and hence Intrapreneurial setup. The mechanism that creates this Intrapreneurial setup however can rest on solid Organizational processes that enable both the environment, governance and Incubation of new business within an Organization.

Please note that I am differentiating here between the actual Incubation of a business vs. the Organizational framework that allows multiple such ideas to originate, take a life of their own and based on performance flourish. This is the true definition in my opinion of an *Innovation Management Function*. This may not be the same as the Research and Development function within an organization.

Why are Intrapreneurs important and why can we not import ideas and then find suitable people to implement them? This is possibly linked to a second question- Can ideas be lifted and wrongly implemented? And I would argue that the idea is as strong as the person who takes charge, simply because the power of the ideas is not just with the ideas themselves, but in the understanding of the ecosystem that makes an idea thrive and provide proper business impetus. There are several risks that can impact the idea negatively and many cultural pitfalls that could completely obliterate it. Within a large Organization then the strength of the Individual and the strength of the organizational framework both come into play when creating an Innovation Ecosystem

Innovation Life Cycle

Innovation Management is as simple or as complex as we make it out to be. The Innovation and Entrepreneurial ecosystem today abounds with words that get into semantics of fine line differences between different stages of Innovation within the Entrepreneurial or Intrapreneurial context. Have I already confused you with the Complexity of words used? Then consider these names of entities that form supportive systems within the Innovation Ecosystem "Incubators, Accelerators, Escalators, Catapults and so on."

To be able to understand the role that these multiple entities play in the Innovation Ecosystem, it is important to understand first the stages of the Innovation Life Cycle. To understand the stages of the Innovation Life Cycle, let us examine the life of an idea from its birth.

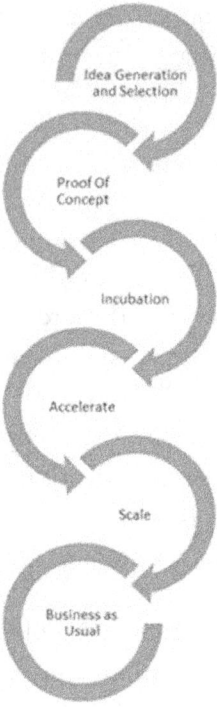

Figure 1. Innovation Life Cycle

The Worthy Idea needs to get created first, sifted through the plethora of ideas that may be popping up around the Organization and then allowed some resources and space for proving the concept behind the idea (Proof of Concept Stage). This is followed by the stage which needs to make the idea commercialization ready. This is usually the Incubation Stage. If the idea is rapidly scalable, then it needs to be provided the support and impetus and market reach through the process of acceleration and escalation. At some point in time the idea becomes mainstream business.

The Idea should be able to get a voice within the Organization. The worthy ideas should be able to be deciphered and selected in the plethora of ideas that may emanate within the Organization.

Once selected, the idea should be able to get enough resources for proving the concept (if there are some points to be considered) and then resources need to be allocated for incubation. If access to certain market parameters including access to real customers is required, then the same needs to be enabled.

Once successfully incubated, the idea needs to go through a stage where its scalability and reach can be ascertained through acceleration and escalation. Subsequently processes need to be put in place so that it is business as usual within the Organization, with the idea having culminated as a new business line, new service, new product or combination of these.

At the bottom-line of these complex processes is the fact that the Innovator should only need to focus on Innovation, the Organizational Enablers in the Form of the Innovation Management function should be able to take care of various parts of these processes, providing an Organizational framework for making things happen.

While we talk of the stages of the Innovation Life Cycle, it is also important to understand that there is a need to address the overall Culture of the Organization and how it needs to be tuned in to these processes.

This discussion cannot really be over unless we discuss probably the most complex part of the process, and that is to determine when an idea/solution is ready for the next stage. Delays in moving from one stage to another could mean critical time to market loss and too early a movement may mean critical inputs relevant to an earlier stage may have missed out, creating product or service which is not optimized for the market

Let us go through each of the Innovation Stages to understand the Organizational Enablers that are relevant and possibly critical to each stage. Refer Figure 1

- Idea Generation and Selection
- Proof of Concept
- Incubation
- Acceleration
- Scale
- Business as usual

Let us now examine the various stages of the Innovation Life Cycle separately and then come back to examine and/or propose the optimum Organizational Enablers for the same

A The Idea Generation and Selection stage: The idea for a new business solution could emerge from within the Organization- from the business teams, from the R&D teams who may have been working on a concept or from the external ecosystems, including the customers, partners etc. There is a need to have systemic methods for capturing these ideas and also enabling some dialogue to happen on such ideas. Enterprise and Partner Social networks can be vital tools for enabling such dialogues to happen. Idea Challenge weeks or days on focussed themes is another method.

I remember getting an Idea Challenge Week being organized in which my company's teams and the Customer teams, both were participants and the Themes for the challenge were based on the Business Imperatives of the Customer Organization. The Selection Committee consisted of people from both Organizations.

While it had taken us some time to convince the Customer to conduct this event, they admitted to being pleasantly surprised with the results. This was Collaborative Idea Generation and Selection at its best.

There has to be a way to get worthy ideas to the topmost level in the organization. The Tata Group organizes an event called Innovista, which is similar to an Idea month, where all Tata Employees can participate. The entries need not be just fresh ideas, but also successful ideas, so that the same can be leveraged as best practices by other companies. And also ideas that were commendable, but failed, the best idea in each category is rewarded.

B. The Proof of Concept Stage: Once an idea has been selected as a worthy idea, and before investment is made for formal incubation, there may be technical, people related or market related assumptions or concepts that may need some experimental validation. The purpose is to outline experimental proof of the concept outlined in the idea proposal. In some cases, this stage may already have been done before the idea validation stage.

C. The Incubation Stage: During this stage the idea is tried end to end in the business environment. If the idea was development of a new solution which sells to the Oil and Gas market, then the incubation stage would involve development, selling and deployment of the solution in at least a couple of customers. Think of the Incubation stage as the "Proof of Concept" of "Go To market".

D. The Acceleration Stage: After successful incubation, there is a need to rapidly assess the overall market potential in all possible allied areas of the solution/product from the idea. E.g. an e-commerce solution developed for Retail may have buyers amongst technology companies selling products to end consumers. The product may be tried in some alternate markets as well. The acceleration stage is more of a "measure of potential stage "and during this stage the investment stage is set for fast scaling up of the solution/ Product idea.

E. The Scaling up: During this stage, based on the assessed potential of the product/solution, Solution scaling up happens. If new markets are targeted, then Internationalization/Localization of the Software product could be part of the Scale investment. The difference between this stage and the business as usual stage, is that the development, marketing, sales and deployment efforts are designed to rapidly scale up with sufficient risk management buffers and governance interventions built into the process.

While every stage is critical, I would like to talk a little bit about the Acceleration and Scale stages of the Innovation Lifecycle. Traditionally businesses have considered the

"Incubation stage" as the most delicate and critical for business success of an Innovation. I am going to argue that it is the Acceleration and the Scale stages that are more critical and more easily messed up today than the Incubation stage. If you pause and think for a while, you will realize that this is probably linked to way the Innovation Life cycle is divided and distributed within the Organization. While there are often functions that support R&D and Idea generation, even Incubation, there is no separate function that is responsible for acceleration and scaling of a solution/business area. In all likelihood this is handled by the Business function which will finally own this directly.

Incubation is difficult, however Incubating and Scaling are 2 different steps. Incubating in a limited environment and demonstrating success may not be able to take into account the additional R&D that may be required for scaling up induced requirements. True, any changes that need to happen further down the innovation life cycle should be anticipated as early as possible, however anybody who has worked on a new product realizes the implications of current and immediate feedback from the market, many of which could not have been envisaged earlier. Having a specifically focussed plan and agenda, with the additional resources lined up, to take care of scaling up challenges on a real time enough basis is extremely critical to the success of such endeavours.

Innovation Management–Nugget No 1- Master the Innovation Lifecycle and establish strong processes for moving from one stage to another effectively

The Innovation adoption Cycle and Technology Readiness

When any company introduces a new product into the market, there is big concern to get the "timing right" for introducing the product. While we all wish we could be psychic when it comes to market projections. In reality it takes a lot of experience and understanding of the market to get this right. In fact a good place to start understanding this is to look at the Innovation Adoption Cycle in Figure 2

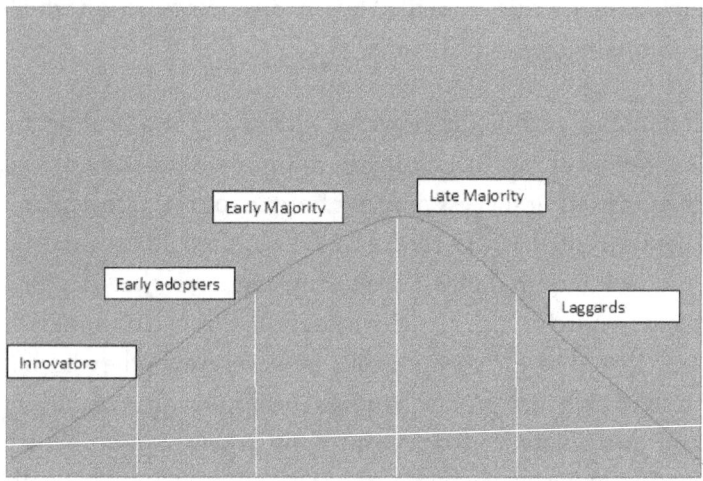

Figure 2: The Innovation Adoption Cycle

When any new innovation or a new technology hits the market, the market usually goes through a gradual acceptance process for the technology or the product. In some rare cases like the Apple iPhone, the acceptance levels rise very quickly across the market, however in most other cases the process is gradual. The Technology or Innovation adoption curve generally looks as in the figure. 3

If you look at the first half of the Innovation adoption Life Cycle curve, and examine a product being introduced into the market before or during the optimum incubation period, the product is likely to get a limited response in the context of the overall market opportunity. If yours is the only product and you had a direct connect to every early adopter, then possibly the product may get some success. This may be true for niche/luxury products. Ide ally the product should hit the market when the early majority begins to make the product popular enough for a sudden increase in market opportunity.

Therefore in Figure 3 you can see that the basic research or the idea validation on a new product/technology/business idea should ideally end before or in the early stages of the ideal incubation period within the Innovation adoption Cycle. This will ensure that there is sufficient time for the product development and go to market to happen, to catch the volume market of the early majority.

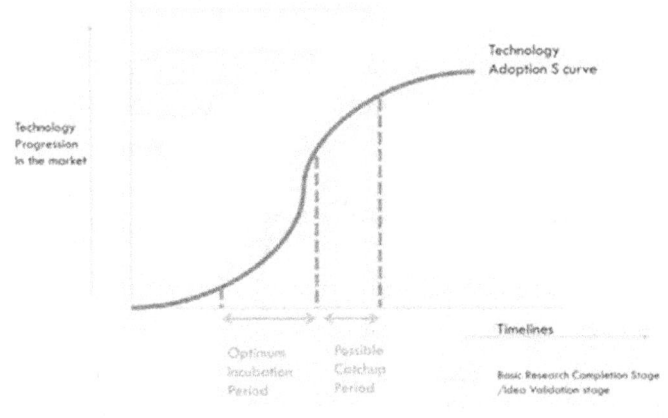

Figure 3

Thus the timing of an Innovation is extremely critical for the marker acceptance of a product or solution.

If I superimpose the Innovation Life Cycle within an Enterprise with the Technology/Innovation adoption Curve, as in Figure 4, it is clear that the Incubation and Acceleration Stages within the Enterprise should ideally coincide with the Optimum Incubation Period for reasonable market success on the Product/Solution launch.

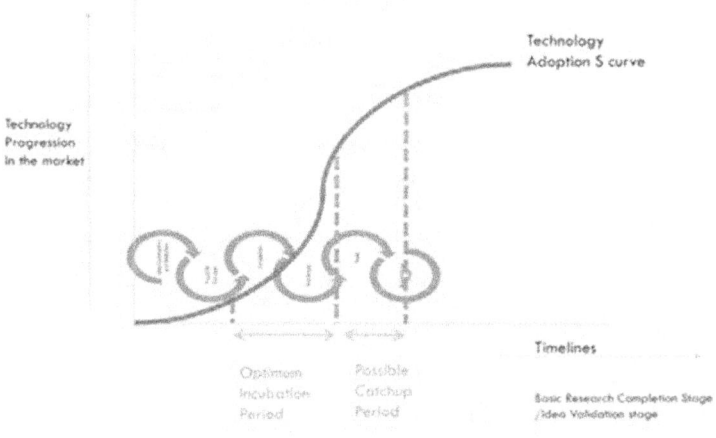

Figure 4: Technology Adoption, Readiness and Innovation Lufe Cycle

The variation across Industries

In order to make sense of the usage of the Innovation adoption cycle in the business environment, it is equally important to understand that the technology readiness stages and duration may be different for different industries.

For example, the technology readiness or idea readiness for launching a new mobile app based on a new business idea may be a few months, now that mobile technology is reasonably mature. However a new design for an airplane engine would a few years to get into production and out in the market. A new material to be part of a new turbine blade in a new engine will take even longer. The market adoption cycles may still be very quick, which means that planning for those industries which have longer duration stages for technology readiness, has to be based on both on the technology readiness curve and the influence that the company may have on the existing market base. Introducing a new technology without an existing customer base is more difficult in such cases.

Innovation Management–Nugget No 2- Plan and Manage Innovation Life Cycles with the Innovation Adoption Cycles of the market to maximize impact

The Concept of the Innovation Ecosystem

Before we talk about Innovation Ecosystems, let me describe what I mean by an Ecosystem –

An Ecosystem is a collective group which impacts and influences the environment in a collective way, while having a stronger correlation and influence on the members of the Ecosystem. The collective group has some special characteristics that makes the impact of this working together greater than the sum of the parts. This is the basic and most simplistic definition of "An Ecosystem". Ecosystems have now become fundamental to fast tracked innovation. A good way to look at an Ecosystem is to consider it as a separate entity which grows/moves forward, with all sub parts moving forward as well.

In the business context Ecosystems could evolve spontaneously or pursued specifically.

A reasonable example of Spontaneous Ecosystem evolution is the case of How a City Evolves. Let's take an example of a city where a particular Industry is extremely rampant, being an IT professional, I am tempted to take the example of Bangalore, the Evolution and Focus on IT and R&D in that region has assumed exponential proportions in the last couple of decades. As the demand for IT professionals grew, the number of Engineering Colleges in the region in and around Bangalore has also grown. Today there are more than a couple of dozen of engineering colleges in and around Bangalore City., leave alone the region around Bangalore and the overall colleges in Karnataka. Similarly the housing requirement for more people migrating to Bangalore to work for the IT companies there, created a strong Infrastructure Business there, so to for Hotels and Restaurants and so on. This is nothing new, this the typical story of how a city's growth gets spiralled. The special characteristic here is the Lead Industry which is driving the rest of the Ecosystem- the Lead Player in the Ecosystem- which is the ICT industry in Bangalore for this case.

On the Other hand a group of disjointed entities may decide to get into a multi member partnership where they are collectively able to influence the market / environment around them with much more force and rigour than they would all be able to do individually. A perfect example of such multi-vendor partnership would be companies which are coming together as partners for overall Internet of Things or Cloud capabilities.

A good example of an Innovation Ecosystem is the Co Innovation Network Ecosystem created by the IT Company Tata Consultancy Services (TCS)

Case Study- The COIN Ecosystem in TCS

Tata Consultancy Services has a Co Innovation Network, where they leverage many players of the External Ecosystem.

These include

- Start-ups
- Academic Institutes
- Alliance Partners

- Research Institutes
- Venture Capitalists
- Industry Bodies
- Customers

Internally the network includes

- TCS Innovation Labs
- Intrapreneurs
- Consultants

While the alliance partners provide the latest technological and solution development support from the large technology companies, the start-ups bring in niche and latest domain, technology, process or market specific capabilities. This combination has the potent capacity to bring cutting edge solutions to the customers, who incidentally are also part of the ecosystem and therefore have some say in the design of the solutions as well. The Venture Capitalists are an important part of the Ecosystem, since their evaluation and association is a measure of the potential and health of the start-up. This is part of the Risk Mitigation Strategy for ensuring that only sustainable solutions are being developed and deployed, and products from start-ups that are more likely to fade out in a couple of years are avoided. Elements of Innovation that come from the Research happening within the TCS Labs, Research Institutes or Academic Institutes could also be part of the solution. The Association with Industry Bodies ensures that specific Interoperability/ compliance standards are understood as part of the solution development process.

In this ecosystem, the Venture Capital firms and the start-ups benefit from the wide customer based reach of TCS, while TCS benefits from taking unique and latest solutions to their customers.

Innovation Management—Nugget No 3: Understand the Ecosystem around your Innovation and establish linkages with ecosystem elements

[1]The Lego Block Approach for Innovation

My son was working on building a helicopter out of lego blocks. Since he is 6 years old, it seemed to me that he would be asking for a lot of help, since the completed model seemed pretty complex, two rotor wings, a central loading area which opened up at the back and allows a small jeep (also made out of lego) to climb in, and side gates that actually open upwards.

I was therefore taken aback when he came to me and with silent pride said " Mom I finally finished making the model, can you please click a photo of me with it" As a mother I was of course thrilled by the fact that he was able to do so on his own. I was however, also intrigued enough to examine the booklet that Lego provided along with the blocks. Aha! The instructions are block by block, module by module building together; each step simple enough itself to be minimally confusing and yet adding to the whole. I was thinking, while this concept is not completely new, yet how wonderful- Isn't this analogous to how we want the building blocks of Innovation to be within a large Organization. The building blocks have to be lego like, each one of them simple enough for anybody in the Organization to pick up and build up and yet all the parts align to form a whole - fitting well into the Organizational Innovation Structure.

As my son was making the model, he would often hunt for that piece which would fit in, and it was kind of scary if a

[1]

particular piece was not being found, since an improvisation with a similar looking block (but not exactly the same) as the one that was required, was likely to cause challenges in later stages of Integration. I felt that there should have been a few extra blocks as backup. Drawing an analogy within the Organizational context, the Risk Mitigations strategies, the redundancies that need to be built into the Frameworks that bind the Innovation functions together are critical.

The Building Block Concept for Development

When people are working and experimenting with ideas and developing something new and there are many unknowns, there is a tendency to build the entire framework, prove that the concept works end to end and then build on top of that. While this is a good approach for development of systems which are well defined, I find the Lego building block approach to be more suitable for development when the outcomes are a little uncertain and I have encouraged teams to use this modular approach. Build a block, make it specific, and yet think of how generic it could be to be used in several scenarios. Build many blocks and through a combination of blocks build different systems. It works!

A company called LittleBits is going one step further and has electronic blocks that allow assembly of small projects. These are great tools used by the educators as well as students to understand electronics and its practical applications.

The entire science of robotics is today based on the concept of small building blocks that can combine to form bigger blocks and so on. . This concept has in fact become the very basis of development of autonomous self-configuring robotic blocks for Space Exploration and Applications

Here are some basic examples to understand what this means

1. Metamorphosis by a self-reconfigurable robot, M-TRAN III at AIST (made by H. Kurokawa)
   The same set of blocks is able to transform itself to different shapes and hence have different uses. The concept is based on simple blocks which combined in different ways to create different kinds of movements and functionality enabling the robot to be able to move across different terrains and around obstacles. Such robots would be extremely for situations where direct feedback and control is not possible, such as for search and report missions in in accessible or dangerous terrain and areas or even space missions.

2. Another good example is the M-blocks robots conceptualized and created in MIT. The robotic blocks are 50mm cubes which are autonomous angular momentum actuated modular robots. The robotic blocks combine through powerful magnets on the faces and edges of the cubes. These modules can jump, rotate, pivot across other cubic blocks and combine to form different shapes and configurations.

Innovation Management—Nugget No 4a: Build organizational elements of Innovation as independent modular building blocks, so that there is enough flexibility in the Innovation Processes.

Innovation Management—Nugget No 4b: Use the building block modular process for Innovation Development, especially if same components of solutions can be used in many solutions

Diversity in Business and its impact on the Innovation Organizational structure

When we are looking at Innovations, we often consider the timeline of impact of the innovation. The impact could be:

- in the short term or the current business,
- in the medium term or next business opportunity
- In the long term or business opportunity for long term sustainability.

These opportunity timeframes are referred to as the 3 time horizons in the context of Innovation Impact.

- **Horizon1:** in the short term or the current business
- **Horizon2:** in the medium term or next business opportunity
- **Horizon3:** In the long term or business opportunity for long term sustainability.

Diversity in Business implies that the three Horizons may map to very different time scales. . Manufacturing intensive industries require major capital investment in Infrastructure as well

Innovation Management—Nugget No 5: Consider the Diversity of your business while creating the organizational Innovation Gears

The Entrepreneur Vs the Intrapreneur

The Merriam Webster dictionary defines the term Entrepreneur as "one who organizes, manages and assumes the risk of business or enterprise"

Dictionary.com defines an Entrepreneur as ""a person who organizes and manages any enterprise, especially a business, usually with considerable initiative and risk."

If you look at the both these definitions, the focus is on organizing and managing risk as if it were your own and on taking initiative.

This is the definition which brings us to the concept of an Entrepreneur within the context of a large organization- Somebody who is now popularly known as an Intrapreneur.

In 1992, The American Heritage Dictionary acknowledged the popular use of a new word, intrapreneur, to mean "A person within a large corporation who takes direct responsibility for turning an idea into a profitable finished product through assertive risk-taking and innovation"

So an Intrapreneur does the same within an Organization that an Entrepreneur does within the gamut of his own company. One may ask "Why is an Intrapreneur important at all" after all there are different people within an organization who manage different things.

The answer probably lies in the speed of Innovation – how quickly are ideas taken to the market. So an Intrapreneur is somebody who will own the organization, managing and risk of a business, while keeping time to market as a key ingredient.

If large Corporates have to innovate at the same rate as startups, then they need to be able to create Opportunities for Intrapreneurship. In the context of large organizations (which have a speed and agility of response different from the startups), this amounts to enabling pockets within the Organization which can move at a faster speed than the rest of the Organization and in an ideal situation at the same speed as that of a startup.

So what are the basic traits that differentiate an Intrapreneur from a regular Employee/Manager/Leader?

- Visionary
  Intrapreneurs like all Entrepreneurs should have Clarity of Vision- Of "What needs to be Accomplished" and Why? Even when everybody is not on board, they have to believe in their vision and have the capacity to enthuse others as well.

- Change Agents
  Intrapreneurs are necessarily change agents. They have the capacity to think beyond the current technological, organizational and environmental framework and enable the change/shift to a radically new scenario

- Risk Aware and Risk Embracing
  Any Entrepreneurial Venture is fraught with risks. The same is true for an Intrapreneurial venture within the Organization. It cannot succeed, if it is just another job. The Intrapreneur has to Understand, Manage and Mitigate the Risks associated with the Venture. The advantage that they do have over and Entrepreneur is that there is much larger Corporate Backing them, and thus many more resources at their disposal to manage this risk more effectively.

  The Risk is a given and has to be embraced and managed rather than avoided.

- Good Leaders
  This is a trait common to Entrepreneurs as well as Intrapreneurs. However, I would argue that the Intrapreneur has to demonstrate stronger Leadership Qualities since he/she needs to manage a much larger set of stakeholders – including those outside as well as inside the Organization

- Passion to "Make a Difference"
  People who are mere managers do not make either good Entrepreneurs or Intrapreneurs. These are driven by a need to succeed and to make a difference. The cause drives them…A new Technology, A new Business Solution or a new way to change the world. The bigger the cause, the more driven the focus.

- Good understanding of the Organizational Dynamics
  One must understand that the Intrapreneur may have a certain degree of freedom akin to an Entrepreneur, yet is still part of a large organization. Being aware of Organizational Dynamics and understanding how it can support or stall the Intrapreneurial efforts is key to the success of such ventures within large organizations. So often an Entrepreneur picked up from outside the organization and given an Intrepreneurial role may not succeed as quickly as envisaged or may fail completely.

Innovation Management—Nugget No 6: Create Opportunities for Intrapreneurship to flourish within the Organization and involve people with Intrapreneurial skills in Incubation and Acceleration

The Culture of Innovation

[Teamwork is the ability to work together
toward a common vision. The ability to direct
individual accomplishments toward organizational
objectives. It is the fuel that allows common
people to attain uncommon results.
[—Andrew Carnegie

Spreading the Culture of Innovation
across the Organization

THE ROLE OF THE THOUGHT INTEGRATORS- THE SOFTER SIDE OF THE INNOVATION SPECIALISTS

In the year 2010 when we started working on what turned out to be a predictive analytics problem for predicting faults in the underground power distribution cables used in India, I realized that the team that we had put together was unable to talk to each other. We had a power sector expert who understood a bit of IT Technology, a Statistical expert, who had worked extensively in healthcare, but never with the Utilities or the Power Distribution problems, we had a couple of hardcore geeks who could solve almost any problem as long as it had to do with bits and bytes (In layman terms, these were solid programmers). The problem statement was clear to all, however it was unclear as to how the team would derive the benefit of the collective experience. This was because of 2 reasons,

1. Nobody understood the subject of the other person well enough to ask the right questions
2. If there was a dispute on some question, answer or even the solution, we did not know how we would solve it

Interestingly I used to be Unix programmer once upon a time, however it had been quite a while since I had to get so close to actual programs being written. As a first step, we created refresher courses (1 day long), and pulled together reading and learning material for people to become familiar with each other's subjects. I realized that since I had a little bit of knowledge of all of these subjects I was able to very quickly act as the central interpreter for all the people in the team. We were able to create a solution that worked. However this whole exercise got me thinking deeply about multidisciplinary knowledge. In the last decade ever since technologies like "cloud" had become more popular, it was becoming increasingly clear to me that the boundaries between subjects were blurring. Look at the solutioning in the cloud context – It requires not just IT Infrastructure knowledge, but also deep knowledge of programming and solutions, SaaS and so on, specially if you are looking at a holistic solution on the cloud. Whenever I discussed this with the people around me, they would turn around and say 'That is why we need Enterprise Architects! This is what an Enterprise Architect is supposed to do"

I was only partially convinced. The Predictive Analytics problems opened up my eyes to the need for people who not only have multidisciplinary capabilities but also the capability to pick up related and unrelated new subjects very quickly. And although it may seem like we are discussing the qualities of a" Jack of all trades", in my experience the only people who fitted the role, were those who had deep knowledge in one or more subjects and also understood a lot of other subjects in some detail. So in some senses we are talking about a "Specialist Generalist". If I keep aside the Subject matter knowledge of this role for a while, it ws very clear that this person is successful in acting as the "Sutradhaar" of the solutioning team only if he/she has the qualities of empathy(being able to understand the other person's viewpoint), Great Communication Skills and Openness to the bizarre. Anything that is not a known truth to us based on our subject matter knowledge seems bizarre to Subject Matter Experts. Does this seem like a bizarre concept?. Logic is defined in the realms of the known and hence any new idea that does not fit into the realm of the known seems bizarre and illogical. All great Innovators are aware of this – the greatest innovations that have disrupted the industry arise from ideas that seem bizarre and difficult to rationalize in the context of the current logic. So these Specialist Generalists need to be able to integrate the Thought Processes from across multiple experts and using their special abilities to devise a composite solution leveraging the combined collective capabilities of the team. I call them the "Thought Integrators"

Looks like we just created a problem for the HR function who has been introduced to a new animal in the corporate woodlands. If we want to institutionalize a culture in which collective Intelligence thrives and where working and solving problems together is valued, then these "Thought Integrators" need to be nurtured, recruited and valued.

Innovation Culture –Nugget No 1- Recruit, Nurture and Value Thought Integrators

Why Collaboration is Important

While we need Thought Integrators or The Specialist Generalists, we also need the leverage of the collective Intelligence of the existing experts within the Organization. This makes practices which promote collaboration extremely important.

Collaboration is important from a diversity in Subject Matter Knowledge Perspective. Even amongst people who seem to have similar Subject Matter Skills, Collaboration may be valuable

When we expose a team of say 10 people to the same problem statement, they come up with variations of answers and approaches to the problem solving. This uniqueness and differences in approach is very valuable from an Innovation perspective. When multiple views are discussed and debated together, then those very brains are led to consider different scenarios, approaches and facts and sometimes derived insights may lead to valuable new ideas. This is an interesting phenomenon, since it put forwards the valuable point, that each individual may have a different set of knowledge base to draw on, since knowledge base is assimilated knowledge and knowledge assimilation is dependent on how we treat the information that we are receiving consciously and sub consciously all the time. This information processing is individually determined for each brain and is what defines the individualism of the person. In a nutshell each person is defined by their life experiences and how they assimilate these…and hence future processing patterns and capabilities are also dependent on the past. While the details of this become a subject of deeper study by the Neurologists and the Sociologists, for us in the Organizational context it is enough to understand that this <u>individually different processing capability of each brain exists and is a power to be drawn upon through Collaboration.</u>

Now that we know that Collective brain power is superior to an Individual's brainpower. We also learnt that the knowledge we assimilate is a result of the exposure to information all around us, in fact the information exposure pattern for each person's life is different...it is a result of the immediate environment of the individual and the life experiences the individual goes through. So the Knowledgebase of each individual is unique. Let's examine another fact- Intelligence is multifaceted and Individuals could manifest higher intelligence in totally different spheres of knowledge/skill.

A corollary to this is the fact that a suitably intelligent multi-skilled team working on a problem collectively should be able to produce a solution /possible solutions that are superior to that of any individual working on it alone. With technology teams, I have observed this phenomenon several times. I have also experienced the exact opposite....where there are several experts in the team and yet the output is not even worth one.

Usually this output is linked to the degree of collaboration in the team. In fact the Concept of leveraging collective intelligence and collective brain power works only when there is collaboration and harmony.

Fundamental rules for successful collaboration

There are some ground rules that will ensure success in collaboration and these become the basis for establishing credibility for collaboration

Rule 1- Collaboration works only if the output is win-win. Some participants in the collaboration ecosystem may gain more, some less, however everyone should gain out of the collaboration effort. It is often the violation of this rule that brings collaboration to a halt. This is nothing new, this is also a fundamental principle for sound business.

Rule 2- Collaboration requires a level of honesty and genuine connect to be really successful. In order to ensure successful collaboration, a level of trust is required between the participants. This can be brought about only with honesty and an ability to connect with each other.

Rule 3- While the fundamental unit of collaboration is linked to human capacity to connect, the dealings/outputs of collaboration need to follow basic business principles where expected roles and responsibilities need to be articulated carefully.

Rule 4- The basic focus for collaboration has to be driven by a higher common agenda for all the participants.

Challenges associated with Collaborative Innovation

When we talk about Collaborative Innovation, I think an important question to ask is whether each individual in the Collaboration Ecosystem believes that they can contribute. Very often than not, Innovation is mistaken to be an R&D function only; In several cases individuals underestimate their own potential of impact in the context of Innovation. "I am not creative", "This is R&D job", "I have a packed schedule- no time for Innovation" and so on. One could effectively address these questions if these are actually asked, however often the underlying thinking is more internalized than externally shared through Corporate Feedback channels and so on. So the Innovation team's challenge is to first uncover and then attempt to dispel all such myths that may be prevalent within the Organizational layers. Another important aspect to consider is that the degree of collaboration possible in a team is dependent on the culture of the group, the mechanisms in place to recognize collaborative efforts and reward those and absence of "Heroes Only will be rewarded" culture. This should not be mistaken to be a promotion of mediocrity, since the star performers tend to leverage the benefit of collaboration to a higher degree in the team (in any case). At the same time everybody benefits from collaboration- net output being higher than one based on individual strengths. The collaboration co-efficient of teams can vary significantly within the same organization, although overall culture does play a role. In this context, getting senior level buy in, sharing important information linked to such team behaviour and the measures to influence it, becomes extremely important.

So when rolling out a Change for Collaborative Innovation, a multipronged approach could help. This implies taking a top down approach as well as bottom up one. Top down- to ensure that a collaborative culture is promoted and Bottom up to encourage individuals to collaborate for Innovation.

Hierarchical Cultures derived from the country of origin could act as deterrent to acceptance of diverse views as well as flow of ideas from the bottom of the Organizational Pyramid to the top of the pyramid, hence special organizational enablers may be required to make this happen.

Innovation Culture –Nugget No 3- Understand the barriers to Collaboration in your Organizational Environment

The Role of Diversity in Innovation

Earlier I mentioned the difference in approach and thinking of people brings different perspective to problem solving. In fact the more diverse the life experiences and learnings of people in the team, more the likelihood of diverse ideas and solutions coming to the fore. A corollary to this is the statement that more diverse teams can be more innovative, provided the culture and environment is supportive of harmonious collaboration.

I have devised a course on "Empowered Creative Thinking" which I have conducted within my Organization for different teams. The one day session includes several experiential learnings through story telling, group exercises and games. I have noticed and validated through observation some very distinct differences in approaches to problem solving in teams of different regions in India and locations outside India. There has to be more data based analysis done to put a full report here, however I would like to mention one observation- the groups that had the most diverse set of people in terms of gender, race, locational experience etc were the ones that came up with the most number of possible solutions to a problem.

Again the role of the Thought Integrators in creating such Diverse Harmonious Collaborative teams becomes useful. Remember we talked about the fact that apart from Subject Matter Knowledge there is today an increased need for people in such roles to have empathy and the capacity to understand, interpret and collate diverse ways of thinking and diverse points of view.

Let us also examine this feature from the point of view of Hierarchical Vs Networked Organizations. The Collaborative approach is naturally supported by networked organizations. These networks can enable linkages beyond the limitations imposed by a strict hierarchy. Since Eastern Cultures tend to be more hierarchical than the West in general, a mix of people from across regions if allowed to set rules of engagement by default, will orient themselves towards a more networked culture.

Innovation Culture –Nugget No 4- Create Environments and promote policies that support Diversity

Mindset for leaders who wish to encourage Innovation

What are the traits of Innovative teams? What creates pockets of high innovation within the same enterprise? Why do pockets of innovation move when some people move? Interesting questions which force you to examine the features associated with such pockets of Innovation and the people who seem to influence a higher degree of innovation. The purpose being that possibly some of the learning's can be applied to create many more such pockets of High Innovation Co-efficient.

Here are some characteristics of High Innovation Teams

1. Passion for Work - Whatever they may be doing
2. Self Belief and Confidence- When one is trying to address a difficult or even a seemingly impossible problem, Confidence and Self Belief is a ground bottom necessity to even move forward. In the absence of "Can do, will do and will prove" spirit, difficult projects are often abandoned. Innovative teams value this Self Belief and Self Confidence in their people and strive to create an atmosphere where such Self Belief and Confidence is not mistaken for Arrogance and snubbed.
3. Curiosity and Questioning Attitude- Innovative people never take anything for granted. They question and question, look for radical ways of doing things (not merely to prove that they are radical, but to find better and quicker solutions).

The underlying belief is that "There has to be a better way to do this. And, if anybody else can find it, why can't I?" Innovative teams understand the inherent motivation driving the questions and hence tend to encourage these. Healthy debates are extremely prevalent amongst such teams.

4. Role of Critics is valued- Innovative teams understand that every idea needs to be subject to the "Critics" view to ascertain that it will really pass the test of business, environment and time. Healthy Criticism is valued and even actively sought. This is easier said than done.....if you examine teams around you, you will really see very few people and few teams who would encourage criticism of any kind.

Leaders need to understand that the Intelligence is multifaceted and individual expression forms for this intelligence are also different. Very often Leaders tend to search for clones of themselves when setting up an optimal team. Actually the most effective team is as diverse as possible- in all sense of that word, however I would like to focus on one or two critical aspects - Diversity of Life Experiences brings in difference in approach to problem solving. Diversity in past professional Experience and Skills implies a difference in Existing Mind Knowledgebase for the Individual and Diversity of Personality again implies a difference in what the person can contribute to the team. The important point to note is that diversity in style needs to be encouraged and critics should be valued

As a Leader, while it may be more challenging to manage a diverse team, if a harmonious team environment gets setup, then Innovativeness of the team could be really high through the leverage of collective potential

Innovation Culture —Nugget No 5- Value the role of the critic

Innovation: Business Alignment: The short term vs long term Conundrum

Innovation is useful to organizations only if it is aligned to Business. Different stakeholders in the organizations are responsible for different business goals in the Organization, some of the goals are short term, others impact business further down the horizon and still others are long term goals. When we discuss the role of innovation in an organization, it needs to be viewed in the context of all these goals (not merely any one of them).

The play out of the business drama in companies is however giving immediate feedback for the short term goals at all times. This is the obvious feedback and is like an action - reaction statement. When short term goals are achieved then there is very tangible outputs and very clear feedback. Positive feedback of this nature is clear, tangible and re-enforces the belief and motivation of people aligned to short term goals. This is required and important....however we now need to shift our attention to the slightly more complex problem of "Impact on Medium term and Long Terms Business Objectives"

If you are responsible for Innovation- You need to understand the impact that Innovation creates for the Long terms goals of the Organization and it will not help if you are looking for, "how many people share the same conviction as you on newly formulated ideas". This also means that as an Innovation Champion you need to be used to hearing conflicting views, valuing them- at the same time, hold the responsibility of standing up to an idea when you believe it has long term potential for the company. This also means that you need to classify the feedback/ viewpoints of the business stakeholders into "Time Horizon" buckets and understand what each of these feedbacks means to you and your Innovation Goals. Stakeholder views on Innovation Subjects are driven by their own goals. So Innovation functions need to make sure that they are taking feedback from a variety of stakeholders and bucket them as short term, medium term and long term impacted stakeholder feedbacks.

Within certain contexts an Innovation that is beneficial to an organization may be seen as a threat to "Spheres of Operation/Influence" for individuals or groups of Individuals who are driven by short term goals, since they may perceive the innovation related Organizational Investments as eating away into their own investment costs. This is not always true, but do remember that an investment that yield results in the medium term or long term cannot and will not fit into the business plan of somebody who is solely focused on short term goals. Yet very often these teams which focus on the short term goals are the ones that are closest to the market and can help get the pulse of the same.

We talked about Time Horizons in an earlier chapter. There is the need to create maps of Time Horizons w.r.t Stakeholder expectations so that the right set of Investors, Influencers and Contributors within the Organization can be leveraged for Innovations that impact different Time Horizons

Innovation Culture –Nugget No 6- Understand who the key Stakeholders are and align long term, medium term and short term innovation objectives with them

Effective teams, Roles and the impact on Innovation

The first question I ask managers /leaders when discussing how to make teams more effective for Innovation is "How well do you know the people in your team?" "Do you know who your key people are and what makes them tick- i.e motivates and de-motivates them?"

Simple Questions? Well, simple for smaller teams....not so simple when applied to large teams. However, knowing the answers to these questions is important not just for Innovation, but for efficient performing teams as well.

High performing teams usually have people working on roles and work that they love. You do not get high performers from roles that do not interest a person. A case in point is a young associate who hated coding and was at the bottom of the performance list. However the same associate was obviously a very "People's person" taking time out to talk and get to know everyone on the team, a regular in social initiatives also in initiatives related to corporate social responsibility, great interest in how the organization functions and very creative. A re-examination of the person's performance keeping in view the outstanding personality traits clearly indicated that the role was a misfit for the person. Thanks to the insight shown by the manager, a role change was initiated and the person soon made a 180 degree switch to a high performer. Alas all managers do not have the same insight into their people or understand the importance of role fitment to take advantage of a person's natural talent and inclinations to get the best out of them.

Another important point to note in such scenarios is to understand that leaders have to try and create win-win prepositions in all scenarios. Every person in the team is unique and his/her value to the Organization is enhanced if the person feels that he/she is adding value and gaining value.

Innovation Culture –Nugget No 7- Know your team's passions, strengths and weaknesses

Innovation - the "This is not Rocket Science" and "I am the expert" Syndrome

Very often business leaders come up with the view- "Is this Innovation?" and that my friends is indeed a good question to ask, one which is valuable in ascertaining the merits of investment made within the Organization. Yet there may often be a certain amount of variation in how this definition is viewed by different people.

Let us look at certain examples to explain what I am saying here.

How would you view the following...are these innovations?

1. The introduction of a new soap with new fragrance and color combination by a FMCG company
2. The discovery of a vaccine for cancer.
3. The introduction of microfinance institutions in India
4. The creation of new robotic technology that enables better open heart surgery
5. The creation of an infinity drive (The Hitchikers Guide to the Galaxy style) which allows unthinkable speeds in space travel.

Now which of the above should be classified as innovations. If you have read the popular innovation books and specially because I am clubbing all of these together - you would pipe up and say- "All of them", yet if I were to ask that question with just the first - Introduction of a new soap by FMCG Company" - many people - specially from the technology world would say- "How is that an Innovation?" The reason why this confusion occurs is largely because of the inability to differentiate Invention and Innovation. While every Invention is an output of Innovation, every Innovation need not be an Invention. A new way of doing something previously known is also an Innovation. The only fundamental requirement from Innovation is that it needs to benefit stakeholders. Yes Innovations are of different kinds -If you are an Innovation practitioner you would already be conversant with the classification for innovation provided by

Prof Clayton Christensen - The terms Disruptive Innovation having been coined by him.http://www.claytonchristensen.com/key-concepts/> Point to note is that all Innovations need not be disruptive...Smaller scale Innovations which Sustain an organizations business by capturing new customers or sustaining loyalty of old customers are equally important for businesses. The other challenge that occurs is because of the fact that there is a difference between having an R&D function and focussing on Innovation. The two are supportive and complementary and yet not necessarily the same. This can be understood better if we try to understand the areas from where Innovation can originate, rather than merely the areas where the first signals to trigger an innovation can come from.

The other point "I am the expert Syndrome" is an interesting one. On one hand we want experts on our teams, on the other we need to be wary that specialization and expertise in one space can sometimes make the best of our people, closed to ideas that come from a different discipline, are contrary to their learnings and so on. This is more of a reminder to the experts themselves to pay attention to the seemingly absurd and illogical, to question to their own hypothesis once in a while, than an indication to Organizations that experts are not desirable on teams

It is important to note that the context of leverage of Collective Capability is dependent on collaboration. So a successful Innovation leader needs to do the following:

1. Understand and leverage the Concept of Multifaceted Intelligence in his team

2. Accept that Diversity is important to Innovation
3. Be willing to "Move out of Comfort Zone" and work with people who may often challenge his views
4. Create a Harmonious Collaborative environment in the team so that collective minds can be applied to problem solving
5. Be extremely clear about rewarding and acknowledging wherever credit for Innovation is due.

That's a difficult list to match in practice and this in turn explains why there are clear pockets of innovation in organizations. It also explains why standard project/program handover/takeovers work in manager roles but not necessarily for leaders in Innovation.

Innovation Culture –Nugget No 8- Value experts but not at the cost of the collective team and it's objectives

Summary

[The essence of many thoughts is in the distillation of the knowledge nuggets]

The Nuggets on Innovation

THE NUGGETS ON INNOVATION

Creativity and Innovation

#1 *Knowledge centric Intuition is important for Business. Use techniques to promote intuitive and "out of the box" thinking*

#2 *The boundaries of science and art and those between subjects are blurring. Recognize this and introduce counterintuitive subject matter expertise into the solutioning discussion to get remarkable results*

#3 *Innovators in Technology can learn from Art and Archaeology. Learning from other subjects can be applied to problem solving in a different subject*

#4 *Get rid of presumptions, expand your thinking, leverage team work and also look for learning from all around.*

#5 *Multidisciplinary knowledge requires some knowledge across multiple subjects. Learning through analogy can help fast track learning in new subjects and analogy derived solutions can be extremely unique and innovative*

The Nuggets on Innovation

Innovation Management

#1 Master the Innovation Lifecycle and establish strong processes for moving from one stage to another effectively

#2 Plan and Manage Innovation Life Cycles with the Innovation Adoption Cycles of the market to maximize impact

#3 Understand the Ecosystem around your Innovation and establish linkages with ecosystem elements

#4a Build organizational elements of Innovation as independent modular building blocks, so that there is enough flexibility in the Innovation Processes.

#4b Use the building block modular process for Innovation Development, especially if same components of solutions can be used in many solutions

#5 Consider the Diversity of your business while creating the organizational Innovation Gears

#6 Create Opportunities for Intrapreneurship to flourish within the Organization and involve people with Intrapreneurial skills in Incubation and Acceeration

The Nuggets on Innovation

Innovation Culture

#1 Recruit, Nurture and Value Thought Integrators

#2 Create an environment for Harmonious Collective Teams and Thought Integration

#3 Understand the barriers to Collaboration in your Organizational Environment

#4 Create Environments and promote policies that support Diversity

#5 Value the role of the critic

#6 Understand who the key Stakeholders are and align long term, medium term and short term innovation objectives with them

#7 Know your team's passions, strengths and weaknesses

#8 Value experts but not at the cost of the collective team and it's objectives

BIBLIOGRAPHY

(n.d.). Reference http:// www.tcs.com/

(n.d.). Reference http://saharaforestproject.com/.

(n.d.). Reference University of Texas: http://www.utdallas. edu/atec/

(n.d.). Reference http://www.ted.com/talks/ryan_holladay_ to_hear_this_music_you_have_to_be_there_literally

(n.d.). Reference http://www.dvice.com/2013-6-10/video-day-sound-waves-create-mesmerizing-patterns-sand

(n.d.). Reference http://www3.imperial.ac.uk/ newsandeventspggrp/imperialcollege/newssummary/ news_2-7-2013-12-26-48

Arbitage, S. (2014, may 14). *In praise of air*. Retrieved from The University of Sheffield: http://www.sheffield.ac.uk

http://en.wikipedia.org/wiki/Sahara_Forest_Project. (n.d.). Retrieved from http://en.wikipedia.org/wiki/.

http://www.designanduniverse.com/articles/high-speed_ trains.php. (n.d.). Retrieved from http://www. designanduniverse.com/.

John W. Romanishin, K. G. (n.d.). *M-Blocks: Momentum-driven, Magnetic Modular Robots*. Retrieved from http://wb.mit.edu: http://web.mit.edu/johnrom/ www/design/publications/M-Blocks,%20Momentum-driven,%20Magnetic%20Modular%20Robots.pdf

Kurokawa, H. (01 June 2007). *Metamorphosis by a self-reconfigurable robot, M-TRAN III at AIST.* Wikipedia, https://unit.aist.go.jp/is/frrg/dsysd/mtran3/.

Lamb, R. (n.d.). Retrieved from http://science.howstuff works.com/.

Roston, A. H. (n.d.). *http://www.bloomberg.com/slideshow/2013-08-18/14-smart-inventions-inspired-by-nature-biomimicry.html.* Retrieved from bloomberg.com.

www.ingramcontent.com/pod-product-compliance
Lightning Source LLC
Chambersburg PA
CBHW071242170526
45165CB00003B/1197